ROBERT RAUSCHENBERG

RETROSPECTIVE

February–April 1984

GALLERIE BEYELER BÄUMLEINGASSE 9 BASEL

PETER BUCHHOLZ, INC.

105 East 16th Street

New York, N.Y. 10003

(212) 477-4622

Hans Peter Adamski

Georg Baselitz

Joseph Beuys

Michael Buthe

Ernst Caramelle

John Chamberlain

Jörg Immendorff

Imi Knoebel

Markus Lüpertz

Palermo

A. R. Penck

Sigmar Polke

Arnulf Rainer

Gerhard Richter

Fred Sandback

Richard Tuttle

Cy Twombly

Robert Wilson

WORKS ON PAPER

ZEICHNUNGEN

L E S   S O I E S

L E S   C R A V A T E S

L E S   F O U L A R D S

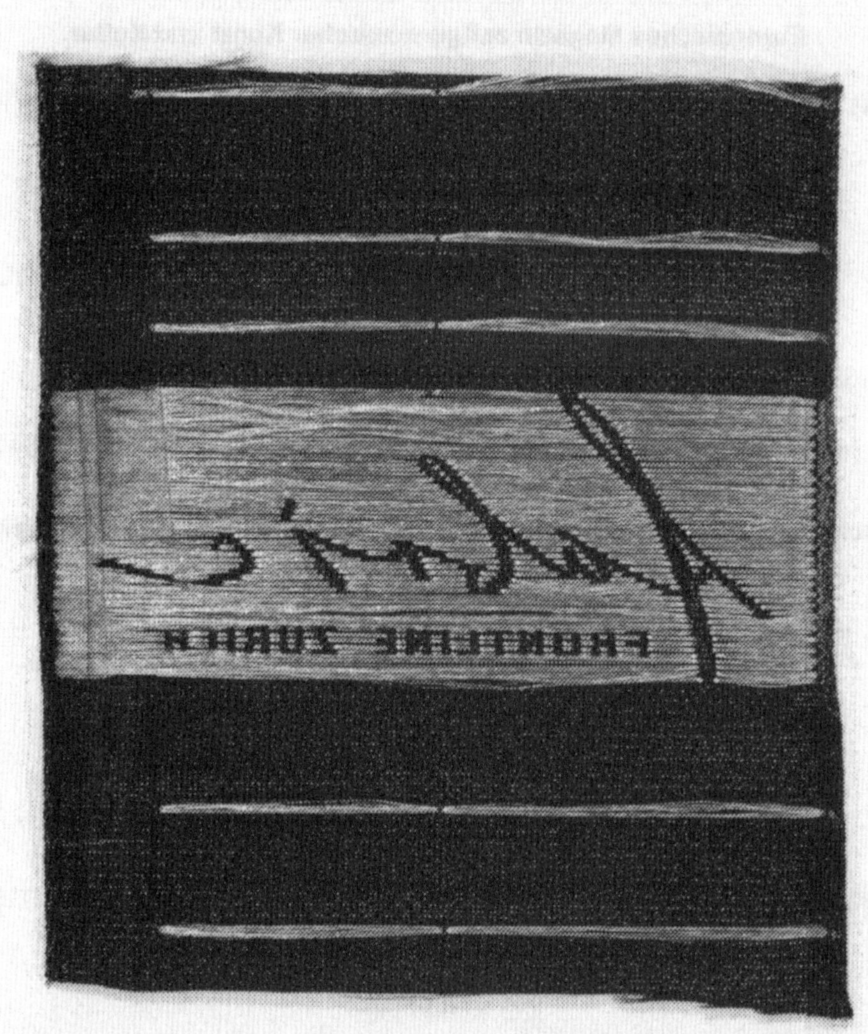

D E   F A B R I C   F R O N T L I N E   Z Ü R I C H   S E E F E L D S T R A S S E   2 9 5 ,   8 0 0 8   Z Ü R I C H

Martin Disler

Bilder

7. März – 27. April 1985

Zur Ausstellung erscheint ein Originalbuch
mit Zeichnungen von Martin Disler
und einem Text von Demosthène Davvetas
in deutscher, englischer und französischer Sprache.

Auflage: 1000 numerierte Exemplare
12 Vorzugsexemplare mit je einer Originalzeichnung

Karl Pfefferle
Galerie & Edition
Maximilianstraße 16
D-8000 München 22 · Tel. 29 79 69

BlumHelman 20 West 57 Street New York

BlumHelman 80 Greene Street New York

Dan Flavin

27 April – 18 May / 420 West Broadway

James Rosenquist

27 April – 18 May / 142 Greene Street

Leo Castelli
New York

VERSO

FALL 1985

Clarence John Laughlin

A MEMORIAL EXHIBITION

Robert S. Zakanitch

NEW PAINTINGS

Jan Groover

PHOTOGRAPHS

George Sugarman

SCULPTURE

ROBERT MILLER 724 FIFTH AVENUE NEW YORK

WINTER 1985/1986

George Sugarman

NEW SCULPTURE

Robert Greene

PAINTINGS

Roberto Juarez

PAINTINGS

Louisa Chase

PAINTINGS

ROBERT MILLER 724 FIFTH AVENUE NEW YORK

EDWARD ALLINGTON

FREDERICK CHILDS

LAUREN EWING

JOEL FISHER

ALLAN McCOLLUM

TONY OURSLER

WADE SAUNDERS

JULIE WACHTEL

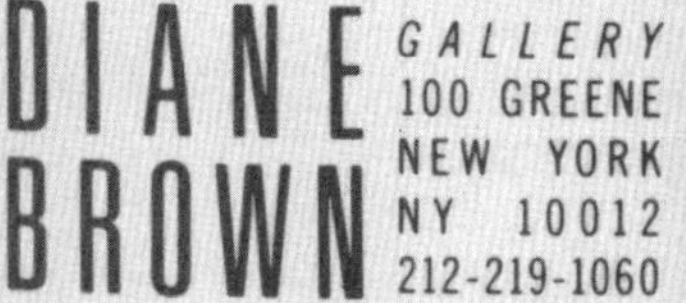

Dieter Teusch

Bilder · Skulpturen

MUNRO

Heilwigstraße 64
2000 Hamburg 20
040/48 45 52 · 47 47 46

8 March-5 April

ROBERT COMBAS
RICHARD SERRA

12 April-3 May

DAVID SALLE
MIQUEL BARCELÓ

10 May-7 June

ROBERT THERRIEN
JOSEPH KOSUTH

LEO CASTELLI
420 West Broadway/142 Greene Street/New York

Changing Group Exhibition

Carl Andre
Jennifer Bartlett
Lynda Benglis
Jonathan Borofsky
Peter Campus
Robert Gober
Robert Grosvenor
Michael Hurson
Donald Judd
Robert Mangold
Elizabeth Murray
Joel Shapiro
Alan Shields
Tony Smith
Robert Wilson
Jackie Winsor

Summer 1986 **Paula Cooper Gallery** 155 Wooster Street New York

LISSON GALLERY

66-68 BELL STREET LONDON NW1 6SP 01-262 1539

LEO CASTELLI

420 WEST BROADWAY / 142 GREENE STREET, NEW YORK

FALL 1986

BRUCE WEBER

LEE KRASNER

RODRIGO MOYNIHAN

RAOUL UBAC

ALICE NEEL

JAMES
BROWN

4-25 OCTOBER

LAWRENCE
WEINER

1-22 NOVEMBER

LEO CASTELLI

420 WEST BROADWAY, NEW YORK

IL CORSO DEL COLTELLO

(THE COURSE OF THE KNIFE)

PROPS COSTUMES AND DESIGNS
BY CLAES OLDENBURG/COOSJE VAN BRUGGEN/FRANK O. GEHRY

CURATED BY GERMANO CELANT

13 DECEMBER-21 JANUARY

LEO CASTELLI
420 WEST BROADWAY, 142 GREENE STREET, NEW YORK

16 APRIL–10 MAY 1987

KENT

41 East 57 Street New York, NY 10022

PETER JOSEPH

23 JUNE–18 JULY 1987

LISSON GALLERY

67 Lisson, Street LONDON NWI 5DA

ULAY/MARINA ABRAMOVIĆ
MARY CARLSON
JAMES CASEBERE
JENE HIGHSTEIN
MATT MULLICAN
PAT STEIR
ROBIN WINTERS
REE MORTON ESTATE

MICHAEL KLEIN, INC.
BROUWERSGRACHT 6, SOU
1013 GW, AMSTERDAM
(020) 26-74-93

MICHAEL KLEIN INC.
611 BROADWAY
ROOM 430
NEW YORK CITY 10012
(212) 505-1980

1957-1987

XXXth

anniversary

leo castelli
new york

zest

fall 1987

Roberto Juarez   Daniel Mahoney
Alex Katz   Ed Ruscha
Ralston Crawford

ROBERT MILLER   41 EAST 57 STREET

FALL 1987

RALPH GIBSON
MIQUEL BARCELÓ
MEYER VAISMAN
RICHARD SERRA
PETER SCHUYFF
EDWARD RUSCHA

LEO CASTELLI
NEW YORK

RICHARD BOSMAN

SEPTEMBER 26-OCTOBER 24, 1987

JOSEPH NECHVATAL

OCTOBER 30-NOVEMBER 28, 1987

ROBERT BORDO

DECEMBER 5-JANUARY 6, 1988

BROOKE ALEXANDER

59 WOOSTER STREET
NEW YORK, NEW YORK 10012
TELEPHONE 212/925-4338

SULKING ROOM

bouder (1) 1 *vi* to sulk, have a sulk *ou* the sulks*. 2 *vt personne* to refuse to talk to *ou* have anything to do with; *chose* to refuse to have anything to do with, keep away from. ils se boudent they're not on speaking terms.

bouderie *nf (etat)* sulkiness *(U)*; *(action)* sulk.

boudeur, -euse *adj* sulky, sullen.

bou•doir *n* [F, fr. *bouder* to pout]: a woman's dressing room, bedroom, or private sitting room

 Advertisements by Artists is a project of Art Metropole, Toronto

10. Okt. – 15. Nov. 1987

Generell

Brigitte Kowanz
Stefan Nessmann
Jörg Schlick
Michael Schuster
Hartmut Skerbisch
Rudi Stanzel
Gustav Troger

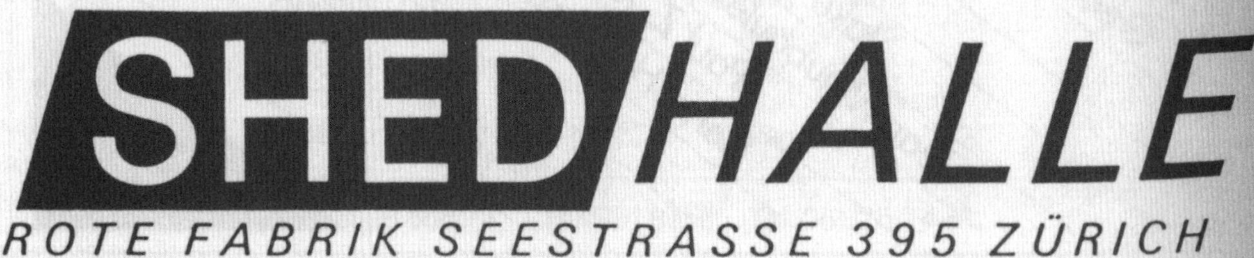

Broken Neon

Albert Oehlen
Martin Kippenberger
Werner Büttner
Bettina Semmer
Georg Herold
Michael Krebber
Georg Jiri Dokoupil
Hubert Kiecol
Josef Beuys
Reinhard Mucha
Meuser
Heimo Zobernig
Jutta Koether
Stefan Nessmann
Markus Oehlen
Günther Förg
Franz West
Fischli & Weiss
Hannes Brunner

20. September bis 11. Oktober '87
steirischer herbst '87 – Forum Stadtpark Graz

GALERIE NÄCHST ST. STEPHAN
ROSEMARIE SCHWARZWÄLDER

JOHN ARMLEDER
HELMUT FEDERLE
FRANZ GRAF
IMI KNOEBEL
GERHARD MERZ
GERWALD ROCKENSCHAUB
NIELE TORONI

GRÜNANGERGASSE 1/2 1010 WIEN/AUSTRIA, TEL. 0222/512 12 66

JOAN MITCHELL

REPRESENTED BY

ROBERT MILLER

41 EAST 57 STREET, NEW YORK

Carl Andre
Jennifer Bartlett
Lynda Benglis
Jonathan Borofsky
Peter Campus
Robert Gober
Robert Grosvenor
Michael Hurson
Donald Judd
Robert Mangold
Elizabeth Murray
Joel Shapiro
Alan Shields
The Estate of Tony Smith
Robert Wilson
Jackie Winsor

Paula Cooper Gallery 155 Wooster New York 212 674.0766

BARBARA GLADSTONE GALLERY

RICHARD PRINCE

APRIL

99 GREENE ST

NEW YORK 10012

212 431 3334

GALERIE NÄCHST ST. STEPHAN
ROSEMARIE SCHWARZWÄLDER

FEBRUAR/MÄRZ

JOSEF ALBERS
JEAN ARP
JOHN McLAUGHLIN

MÄRZ/APRIL

DONALD JUDD

GRÜNANGERGASSE 1/2 1010 WIEN/AUSTRIA, TEL. 0222/512 12 66

ANTONY GORMLEY

APRIL 7 — MAY 14, 1988

DENZIL HURLEY

MAY 20 — JUNE 18, 1988

FRANZ ERHARD WALTHER

JUNE 24 — JULY 30, 1988

BURNETT MILLER
GALLERY
[illegible]4 NORTH LA BREA AVENUE
LOS ANGELES, CALIFORNIA 90038
[illegible] • 874-4757

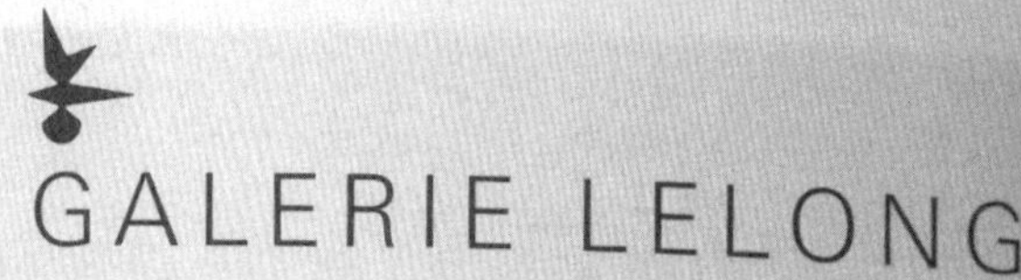

GALERIE LELONG

PARIS

13 + 14, RUE DE TÉHÉRAN PARIS 8e TEL. 4 563 13 19

26 MAI – 30 JUIN

ADAMI

ZÜRICH

PREDIGERPLATZ 10 – 12 8001 ZÜRICH TEL. 01 251 11 20

MAI

LÜPERTZ

BILDER + ZEICHNUNGEN

CHILLIDA

18. JUNI – 31. JULI

NEW YORK

20 WEST 57 STREET 5TH FLOOR NEW YORK NY 10019 TEL. 212 315-0470

MAY – JUNE 4

GROUP SHOW

ROSS BLECKNER, PETER HALLEY, SHERRIE LEVINE, PHILIP TAAFFE, JAMES WELLING, CHRISTOPHER WOOL

JUNE 9 – JULY 15

JUSTEN LADDA

SIMULATION MELTDOWN

GALERIE NÄCHST ST. STEPHAN
ROSEMARIE SCHWARZWÄLDER

AI

SHERRIE LEVINE

UNI/JULI

ERNST CARAMELLE

GRÜNANGERGASSE 1/2, 1010 WIEN/AUSTRIA, TEL. 0222/512 12 66

Louise Bourgeois

REPRESENTED BY

ROBERT MILLER

41 EAST 57TH STREET NEW YORK

JANUARY

KEITH SONNIER

FEBRUARY

RICHARD ARTSCHWAGER

MARCH

ROY LICHTENSTEIN

LEO CASTELLI

420 WEST BROADWAY NEW YORK

6-22 December 1988

Changing Group Exhibition

January 1989

Michael Hurson

January

Robert Gober

February

Paula Cooper 155 Wooster Street New York 212 674.0766

“SONGLINES”

JANUARY

JAMES CASEBERE

FEBRUARY

GERRY MOREHEAD

MARCH

January

Keith Sonnier

Work from the 1960s

in
cooperation
with

Leo Castelli

BARBARA GLADSTONE GALLERY
99 Greene Street
New York, New York
10012
212 431 3334
Fax 212 966 9310

KATE ERICSON

MEL ZIEGLER

7 JANUARY THROUGH 11 FEBRUARY 1989

BURNETT MILLER
G A L L E R Y
964 NORTH LA BREA AVENUE
LOS ANGELES, CALIFORNIA 90038
213·874-4757

THERESE OULTON

FEBRUARY 1989

HIRSCHL & ADLER Modern

851 Madison Avenue
New York, New York 10021
212 744-6700
FAX 212 737-2614

JEFF KOONS

His signature points to:

Discretion, diplomacy, a lack of desire to reveal his true self but also strong individualism, a sense of independence, his ability to stand by himself and much originality. He possesses excellent energy and the determination to carry out his plans and projects, utilizing whatever means to reach his goal. He throws himself into his work, and his day-by-day activities are more important than other aspects of his life. In his efforts he is assisted by his critical perceptions and his creative imagery, a feeling for color, form and space that are evident in his work. To-date he is still involved in an internal struggle to refine his personal style and find his position (or better establish himself securely) for a greater freedom of expression of his talents.

He himself is impetuous, frequently carried away by his impulses and his stubbornness that brooks no interference with his preferences, plans or personal tastes. He may appear to be egotistical, self-involved, "above the crowds", indicating a narcissistic streak. Yet, at times, he displays a certain amount of largesse and magnanimity toward those he likes, and he can be generous to his friends, ready to invest in causes in which he believes.

Despite his sophistication and less than provincial interests, he does not permit easy access in intimate situations or personal relationships, and it would take much time and effort to break down his emotional distance. He must be given credit for having pulled himself up by his own boot straps from a less than secure past through hard work to acquire his present day knowledge. While sometimes he is still tempted to return to his past (or allow old memories to haunt him), he struggles to liberate himself from old insecurities through his work, and he utilizes his artistic talents to live in the present, further projecting himself to a more rewarding and secure future.

Look at the signature again. It looks like a stylized bird soaring in the air, free from constraint . . . !

Handwriting Analysis By:

HERRY O. TELTSCHER, PH.D.
CERTIFIED PSYCHOLOGIST
GRAPHO-DIAGNOSTICIAN

SONNABEND 420 WEST BROADWAY NEW YORK

JEDD GARET

McDERMOTT & McGOUGH

MARCH

ROBERT MILLER 41 E 57 NEW YORK

February 25 - March 25, 1989

REPETITION

Carl Andre
Giovanni Anselmo
Donald Baechler
Bernd and Hilla Becher
Joseph Beuys
Mel Bochner
Marcel Broodthaers
Richmond Burton
Scott Burton
Hanne Darboven
Christian Eckart
Dan Flavin
Gilbert and George
Jochen Gerz
Rebecca Horn
Jasper Johns
Donald Judd
Ange Leccia
Sol Lewitt
Richard Long
Piero Manzoni
Brice Marden
Gerhard Merz
Marilyn Minter
Robert Morris
Bruce Nauman
Giulio Paolini
Sigmar Polke
Robert Rauschenberg
Peter Roehr
Haim Steinbach
Rosemarie Trockel
Andy Warhol
Chris Wilmarth
Christopher Wool
Joe Zucker

HIRSCHL & ADLER Modern

851 Madison Avenue
New York, New York 10021
212 744-6700
FAX 212 737-2614

Catalogue available $20.

DOKOUPIL

SEPTEMBER 1989
ROBERT MILLER GALLERY
41 EAST 57 NEW YORK
IN COOPERATION WITH LEO CASTELLI

GÜNTHER FÖRG
CRISTINA IGLESIAS
ETTORE SPALLETTI
JAN VERCRUYSSE
FRANZ WEST
CHRISTOPHER WOOL

JOOST DECLERCQ - *GENT*
MAX HETZLER - *KÖLN*
LUHRING AUGUSTINE - *NEW YORK*
PETER PAKESCH - *WIEN*
MARGA PAZ - *MADRID*
MARIO PIERONI - *ROMA*

SUMMER 1989

ROBERT GREENE

PAINTINGS

ANDY WARHOL

PHOTOBOOTH PICTURES

ROBERT MILLER 41 EAST 57 NEW YORK

PARKETT ADS brings together a collection of gallery advertisments published in Parkett, a seminal art magazine issued between 1984 and 2017. Tiane Doan na Champassak selected spreads from the first 22 issues of the magazine.

Editorial coordination: Miléna Chevillard
Publisher: RVB BOOKS, Matthieu Charon, Rémi Faucheux

ISBN 978-2-492175-49-7
Achevé d'imprimer en juillet 2024.
Dépôt légal : juillet 2024